Grade 3

Carson-Dellosa Publishing LLC
Greensboro, North Carolina

Credits
Content Editor: Amy R. Gamble
Copy Editor: Angela Triplett

Visit **carsondellosa.com** for correlations to Common Core, state, national, and Canadian provincial standards.

Carson-Dellosa Publishing LLC
PO Box 35665
Greensboro, NC 27425 USA
carsondellosa.com

© 2019, Carson-Dellosa Publishing LLC. The purchase of this material entitles the buyer to reproduce worksheets and activities for classroom use only—not for commercial resale. Reproduction of these materials for an entire school or district is prohibited. No part of this book may be reproduced (except as noted above), stored in a retrieval system, or transmitted in any form or by any means (mechanically, electronically, recording, etc.) without the prior written consent of Carson-Dellosa Publishing LLC.

Printed in the USA • All rights reserved.

ISBN 978-1-4838-5017-7
01-312181151

Table of Contents

Introduction 4
Developing Problem-Solving Skills 5
Tracking Problem-Solving Skills 6
Standards Alignment Chart 7
School-to-Home Connection 8
Week 1: Circle the Important Numbers 9
Week 2: Underline and Understand the
    Question 11
Week 3: Box the Key Words 13
Week 4: Eliminate the Extra
    Information 15
Week 5: Solve and Check Your
    Answer 17
Week 6: Use the CUBES Strategy 19
Week 7: Use a Graph 21
Week 8: Find a Pattern 23
Week 9: Use Place Value 25
Week 10: Use a Bar Model with Parts of a
    Whole 27
Week 11: Use a Bar Model for
    Comparison 29
Week 12: Act It Out (Multiplication) 31
Week 13: Draw a Picture (Arrays) 33
Week 14: Write a Number Sentence 35
Week 15: Use a Symbol for the
    Unknown (Multiplication) 37
Week 16: Restate the Problem in Your
    Own Words 39
Week 17: Guess and Check 41
Week 18: Use the CUBES Strategy 43

Week 19: Solve a Simpler Problem 45
Week 20: Act It Out (Division) 47
Week 21: Write a Number Sentence 49
Week 22: Use Logical Reasoning 51
Week 23: Work Backward 53
Week 24: Make an Organized List 55
Week 25: Make a Table 57
Week 26: Break the Problem into
    Smaller Parts 59
Week 27: Draw a Picture (Fractions) 61
Week 28: Use a Number Line
    (Fractions) 63
Week 29: Use a Bar Model with
    Equal Parts 65
Week 30: Use a Conversion Chart 67
Week 31: Use a Formula 69
Week 32: Draw a Diagram 71
Week 33: Use a Number Line
    (Elapsed Time) 73
Week 34: Use Estimation 75
Week 35: Use a Symbol for the
    Unknown (Measurement) 77
Week 36: Use a Logic Grid 79
Week 37: Draw a Picture
    (Measurement) 81
Week 38: Make a List and Eliminate 83
Week 39: Use Equivalent Fractions 85
Week 40: Use the CUBES Strategy 87
Answer Key 89

Introduction

Problem Solving 4 Today: Daily Skill Practice is a comprehensive yet quick and easy-to-use supplement to any classroom math curriculum. This series will strengthen students' problem-solving skills as they review and use strategies to solve word problems in numbers, operations, algebraic thinking, measurement, data, and geometry.

This book covers 40 weeks of daily problem-solving practice. Essential problem-solving skills are practiced each day during a four-day period with a problem-solving strategy introduced at the beginning of each week. Students are encouraged to solve the problems each day using the specified strategy. On the fifth day, an assessment is given to allow students to prove their competency in using the weekly strategy. Although the strategies are presented in a consecutive format, they can be used in any order.

Various problem-solving skills and strategies are reinforced throughout the book through activities that align to state standards. To view these standards, see the Standards Alignment Chart on page 7.

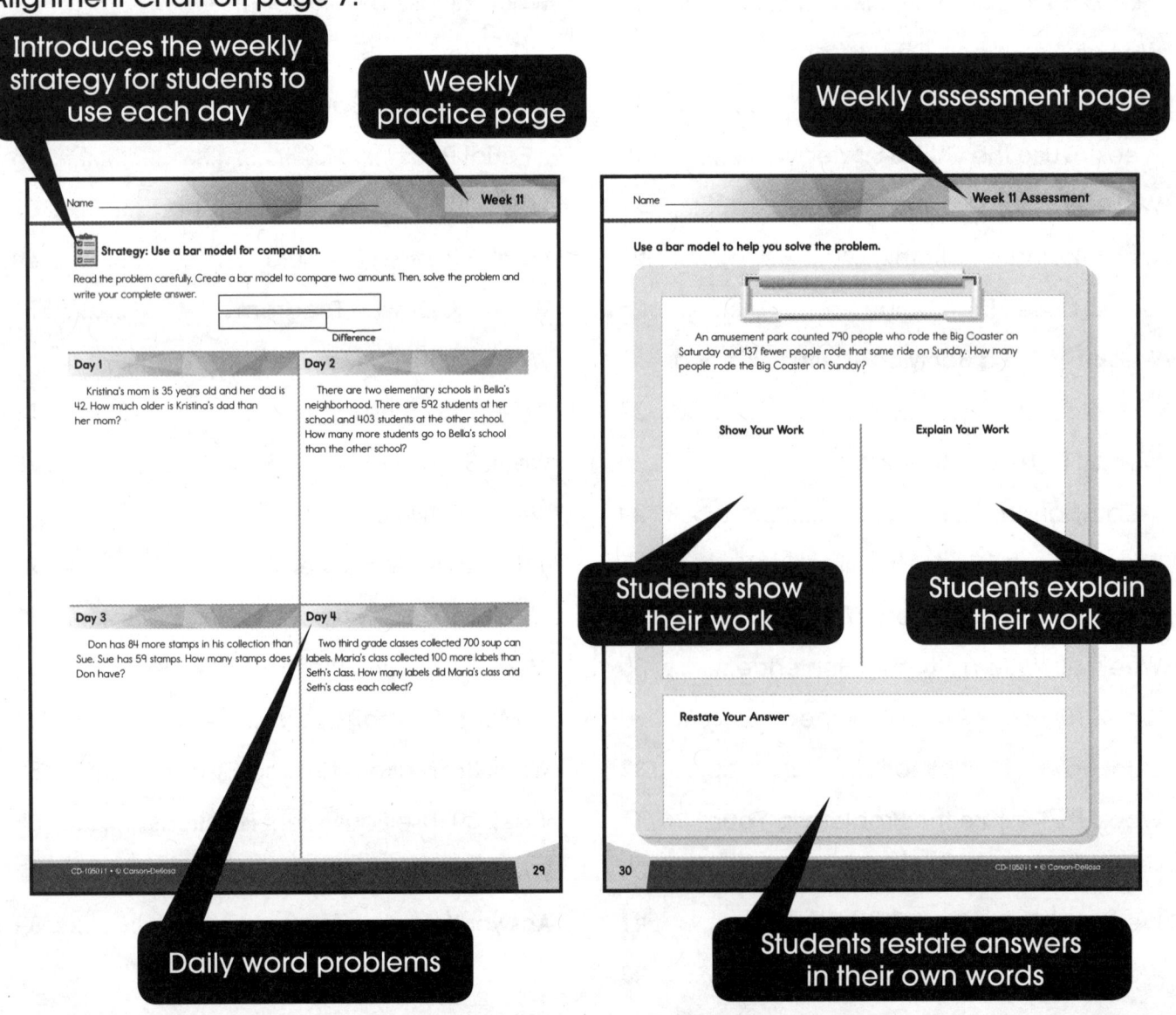

Developing Problem-Solving Skills

Solving word problems is an essential skill that every student must master. Developing and practicing problem-solving strategies enables students to deal more effectively and successfully with most types of mathematical problems.

With this series, a word problem will be presented each day for students to solve using a strategy that is intended to work well with the problem. Teachers should review and discuss the strategy and its applications at the beginning of each week. The word problems can then be given as part of a morning work routine, given as a nightly homework assignment, used in math journals, or cut apart and placed in a math center. The weekly assessment page is useful to have students show the steps they took to solve the word problem and to explain their reasoning.

The Problem-Solving Process

When solving math problems, students should be encouraged to follow this general problem-solving process as well as to develop and use their own problem-solving strategies.

Understand
- Restate the problem in your own words.
- What facts/information/data are given?
- What are you being asked to find?
- What information is missing or not needed?

Plan
- Which strategy should I use?
- Have I solved similar problems before?

Act
- Implement a strategy.
- Check each step of the plan as you work it.

Reflect
- Have you answered the question?
- Is the answer reasonable and accurate?
- Can you find another method or work backward to check your work?

Tracking Problem-Solving Skills

Have students use the reproducible on page 6 to keep track of their understanding of solving word problems. Four times during the year, have students complete the first column by adding the date and then drawing the appropriate symbol for each I Can . . . statement using the key under the chart. Repeat several times to show progress throughout the year. Have students answer the prompts at the bottom of the page to assess their overall learning.

Tracking Problem-Solving Skills

Name _____

Skill	Date	Date	Date	Date
I can choose the correct operation.				
I can identify key words.				
I can use a variety of strategies.				
I can solve multistep word problems.				
I can explain my answer.				
I can solve word problems with fractions.				
I can solve word problems involving area.				
I can solve word problems involving converting measurements.				
I can solve word problems involving perimeter.				
I can solve word problems involving mass and volume.				
I can solve word problems involving picture and bar graphs.				

Ratings   ✗ = not yet   ? = maybe   ✓ = yes

One thing I understand well is   One thing I can improve on is

Standards Alignment Chart

State Standards*		Weeks
Operations and Algebraic Thinking		
Represent and solve problems involving multiplication and division.	3.OA.1–3.OA.4	12, 13, 15–21, 26, 31, 32
Understand properties of multiplication and the relationship between multiplication and division.	3.OA.5, 3.OA.6	15
Multiply and divide within 100.	3.OA.7	12–16, 20, 21, 31
Solve problems involving the four operations, and identify and explain patterns in arithmetic.	3.OA.8, 3.OA.9	1–8, 10, 11, 14, 16–18, 23, 25, 29, 35, 40
Number and Operations in Base Ten		
Use place value understanding and properties of operations to perform multi-digit arithmetic.	3.NBT.1–3.NBT.3	9, 18, 19, 22, 26, 29, 30, 38
Number and Operations—Fractions		
Develop understanding of fractions as numbers.	3.NF.1–3.NF.3	27–29, 32, 39
Measurement and Data		
Solve problems involving measurement and estimation.	3.MD.1, 3.MD.2	17, 26, 30, 33, 34, 40
Represent and interpret data.	3.MD.3, 3.MD.4	7, 24, 25, 36
Geometric measurement: understand concepts of area and relate area to multiplication and to addition.	3.MD.5–3.MD.7	26, 31, 32, 37
Geometric measurement: recognize perimeter.	3.MD.8	31, 32, 37
Geometry		
Reason with shapes and their attributes.	3.G.1, 3.G.2	8, 26, 36–38

* © Copyright 2010. National Governors Association Center for Best Practices and Council of Chief State School Officers. All rights reserved.

School-to-Home Connection

The research is clear that family involvement is strongly linked to student success. Support for student learning at home improves student achievement in school. Educators should not underestimate the significance of this connection.

The skill-building format of this book creates an opportunity to expand this school-to-home connection. Students are encouraged to practice their word problem-solving skills at home. Parents and guardians can use the reproducible strategy sheet (below) to help their students solve word problems at home during the week. The CUBES chart can also be used in the classroom by posting it in a math center or allowing students to glue it into their math journals.

In order to make the school-to-home connection successful for students and their families, it may be helpful to reach out to them with an introductory letter. Explain the problem-solving process and the CUBES strategy. Encourage them to offer suggestions or feedback along the way.

CUBES Problem-Solving Strategy

C — Circle the numbers.
U — Underline the question.
B — Box the key words.
E — Eliminate extra information. Evaluate: What steps do I take?
S — Solve and check.

Name _____ Week 1

 Strategy: Circle the important numbers.

Read the problem carefully. Circle the numbers you will use to solve the problem. Then, solve and write your complete answer.

Day 1

Charlie's mom ordered 48 balloons for his birthday party. She tied 12 of the balloons to the mailbox. How many balloons are left to decorate inside the house?

Day 2

Sydney collected bottles to recycle to raise money for her school. In September, she collected 26 bottles, and in October, she collected 31 bottles. How many bottles did she collect altogether?

Day 3

A comic book store has 85 comic books and 50 action figures. How many more comic books does the store have than action figures?

Day 4

The two third-grade classes at Carter Elementary collected cans for a food drive. Ms. Brown's class collected 64 cans and Mr. Wen's class collected 34 cans. How many total cans did the third grade collect?

Name _____   **Week 1 Assessment**

Circle the important numbers to help you solve the problem.

Lauren sells raffle tickets for a charity event for the 8th Street Youth Center. She only sells tickets to two people. Her mother buys 28 raffle tickets and her neighbor Ms. Jordan buys 21 raffle tickets. How many tickets did Lauren sell?

Show Your Work

Explain Your Work

Restate Your Answer

Name _____   Week 2

 Strategy: Underline and understand the question.

Read the problem carefully. Underline the question and think about what it is asking you to do or find. Then, solve and write your complete answer.

Day 1

A zookeeper weighs the animals in the Australian section of the zoo. The kangaroo weighs 89 pounds and the koala bear weighs 12 pounds. Which animal weighs more and by how much?

Day 2

Carlos has a jar of marbles. In the jar, there are 33 blue marbles and 56 green marbles. How many marbles does Carlos have?

Day 3

Harper has a lemonade stand. She buys enough lemonade mix to make and sell 75 glasses. On Saturday, she sold 34 glasses. How many glasses of lemonade can she make and sell on Sunday?

Day 4

Devin has a summer paper route. He makes $44 in June and $55 in July. How much money has Devin made by the beginning of August?

Name _____   **Week 2 Assessment**

Underline and understand the question to help you solve the problem.

Cameron and her brother are collecting pennies to make 50-cent rolls. Cameron filled 4 rolls and has 36 pennies left. Her brother says he'll give her some of his pennies to make another complete roll. How many pennies should Cameron's brother give her?

Show Your Work

Explain Your Work

Restate Your Answer

Name _____ Week 3

 Strategy: Box the key words.

Read the problem carefully. Box the key words that tell you what operation to use to solve the problem. Then, solve and write your complete answer.

Day 1

Felicia and Reggie were racing to see who could read the new book in their favorite series first. By the end of the first week, Felicia had read 16 more pages than Reggie. If Reggie had read 72 pages, how many pages did Felicia read?

Day 2

The City Aquarium got a new jellyfish tank and a new penguin exhibit. The jellyfish tank has 87 jellyfish and the penguin exhibit has 43 penguins. How many more jellyfish does the aquarium have than penguins?

Day 3

Joyce got a new box of 100 colorful paper clips. She gives all 25 red paper clips to her friend for a project. How many paper clips does Joyce have left?

Day 4

A bird watcher counted 29 birds in his backyard. Then, 8 more birds flew in to join them. How many birds were in the backyard in all?

Name _____   **Week 3 Assessment**

Box the key words to help you solve the problem.

The school counted the textbooks at the end of the school year. They counted 163 math books, and then they found 17 more in another classroom. How many math books will the school have in all for the start of the new school year?

Show Your Work

Explain Your Work

Restate Your Answer

Name _____ Week 4

 Strategy: Eliminate the extra information.

Read the problem carefully. Cross out extra information that is not needed to solve the problem. Then, solve and write your complete answer.

Day 1

Mr. Stone's class is having Family Fun Night with a goal to raise $100. Students win prizes from points earned at 6 different games. Students need 26 points to win a key chain and 42 points to win a yo-yo. How many more points does it take to win a yo-yo than a key chain?

Day 2

At the Snack Shack, a granola bar costs 30¢, a banana costs 25¢, and a juice box costs 65¢. Ling has $3.00 to spend. She buys a granola bar and a juice box. How much did Ling spend in all?

Day 3

Gia needs seashells for a science project that's due in 2 weeks. She has 57 shells. Her aunt sent her 26 more. She still needs 15 more shells. How many shells does Gia have?

Day 4

Colin is saving for a theme park ticket. An adult ticket costs $75, a child ticket costs $40, and a senior ticket costs $25. Colin has saved $18 already. His friend has saved $26. How much more does Colin need to save before he can buy a child ticket?

Name _____   **Week 4 Assessment**

Eliminate the extra information to help you solve the problem.

Anna and Maya have both been playing basketball for 3 years. This season, their team won 19 games, lost 7 games, and tied 6 games. How many games did their team either win or tie this season?

Show Your Work

Explain Your Work

Restate Your Answer

Name _____ Week 5

 Strategy: Solve and check your answer.

Read the problem carefully. Solve and check to make sure your answer makes sense. Then, write your complete answer.

Day 1

Nico owns a furniture store and adds up a bill of $498 for a new client. The client ordered a desk for $355 and a matching chair. How much did the chair cost?

Day 2

Diana works at the ice-cream shop and tracks the total number of scoops sold each day. One weekend, she sold 511 scoops on Saturday and 204 scoops on Sunday. How many ice-cream scoops did Diana sell in all over the weekend?

Day 3

Emma is ordering beads to make necklaces. She needs 275 pink beads and 150 pearl beads. What is the total number of beads that Emma needs?

Day 4

An electronics store was having a sale. Bryce bought a camera that originally cost $216. The discount on the camera was $63. How much did Bryce pay for the camera?

Name _____

Week 5 Assessment

Solve. Then, check your answer to make sure it makes sense.

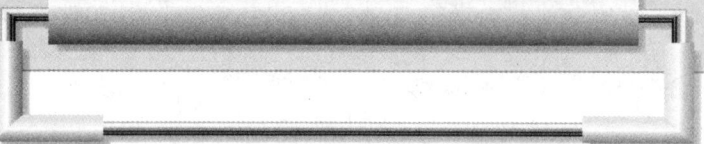

Best Books sells used books. The staff spent the weekend taking inventory. They counted 481 fiction books and 349 nonfiction books. If the owner of Best Books wants to have the same number of nonfiction books as fiction books, how many more used nonfiction books does he need to buy?

Show Your Work

Explain Your Work

Restate Your Answer

Name _____ **Week 6**

 Strategy: Use the CUBES strategy.

Read the problem carefully. **C**ircle the important numbers. **U**nderline the question. **B**ox the key words. **E**liminate extra information. **S**olve and check your answer.

Day 1

Demarco runs 4 to 5 times a week. He runs 5 kilometers on some days and 8 kilometers other days. Last week, Demarco ran for 150 minutes and this week he ran for 139 minutes. How many more minutes did Demarco run last week than this week?

Day 2

The middle school band planned two concerts at the school. There are 73 musicians and 18 singers. The band sold 834 tickets for the first show and 692 tickets for the second show. If they need a program for every ticket sold, how many programs should they print?

Day 3

Neva is making keychains for the craft fair. She wants to have 200 keychains to bring to the fair. She uses 346 inches of cord to make the keychains. If a spool of cord is 500 inches long, how much cord does Neva have left?

Day 4

An art museum sells postcards for 79¢ each. There are 963 modern art postcards, 452 Renaissance art postcards, and 758 Impressionist art postcards. How many more postcards show modern art than Impressionist art?

CD-105011 • © Carson-Dellosa   19

Name _____

Week 6 Assessment

Use the **CUBES** strategy to help you solve the problem.

Students in the science club are selling two types of calendars. They sold 218 space calendars and 192 animal calendars. The science club made $463 from the space calendars and $288 from the animal calendars. How much money did the science club make in all?

Show Your Work

Explain Your Work

Restate Your Answer

Name _____

Week 7

 Strategy: Use a graph.

Read the problem carefully. Use the graph to solve the problem. Then, write your complete answer.

Day 1

The ice-cream truck sold five flavors of frozen treats throughout the day. Which three flavors were sold the least?

Frozen Treat Flavors Sold

Type of Frozen Treat	
grape	🍧 🍧
orange	🍧 🍧 🍧 🍧 🍧
cranberry	🍧 🍧 🍧
cherry	🍧 🍧 🍧 🍧 🍧
strawberry	🍧 🍧 🍧

Number of Frozen Treats Eaten
🍧 = 10 frozen fruit treats

Day 2

Karla tracked the weather last month. How many more days were sunny than rainy?

Weather Last Month

Type of Weather	
sunny	☁☁☁☁☁
windy	☁☁☁☁☁☁☁☁☁
rainy	☁☁☁☁
cloudy	☁☁☁☁☁☁☁

Number of Days
☁ = 2 days

Day 3

Malik graphed the votes students received for class president. How many fewer votes did the student with the least number of votes get than the election winner?

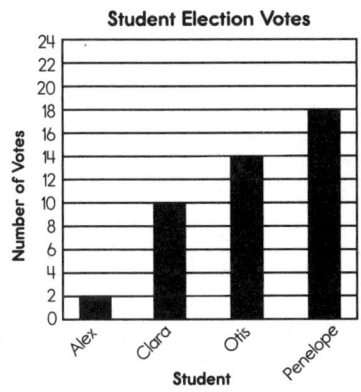

Day 4

Mrs. Hayes keeps track of her students' birthdays by season to see how many birthday pencils to buy each season. How many students have birthdays during the school year?

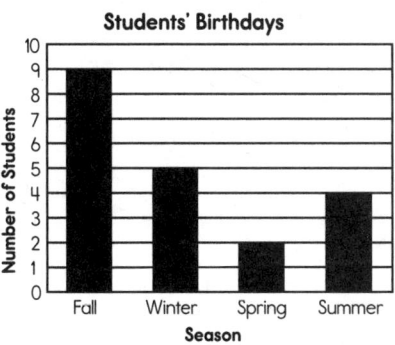

Use the graph to help you solve the problem.

Harrison asked students in his grade what their favorite colors were. He displayed his results on a bar graph. How many more students chose the three most popular colors than those who chose the three least popular colors?

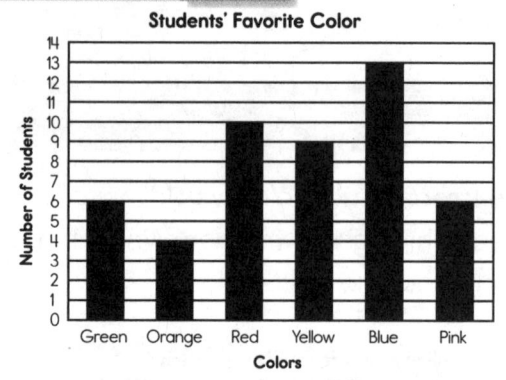

Students' Favorite Color

Show Your Work

Explain Your Work

Restate Your Answer

Name _____   Week 8

 **Strategy: Find a pattern.**

Read the problem carefully. Find a pattern to solve the problem. Then, write your complete answer.

Day 1

Hana added a border to the top of her poster with dot stickers using the pattern below. How many more dot stickers will she need to complete the patterned border?

oo oo oo oo oo ___ ___ ___
    oo   oo

Day 2

Manuel made a pattern with the shapes below. How many sides were there in all in his pattern?

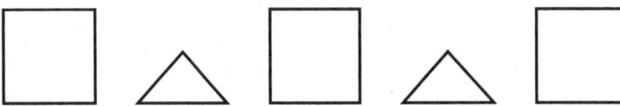

Day 3

David noticed that the numbers in a column of a hundreds chart made a pattern. Use the pattern he saw to write the next 7 numbers in that column.

1	2	3	4	5	6	7	8	9	10
11	12	13	14	15	16	17	18	19	20
21	22	23	24	25	26	27	28	29	30

4, 14, 24, ____, ____, ____,
____, ____, ____, ____

Day 4

Tina started at 30 and counted backward by fives. How many numbers did she say before getting to 0?

Name _____   **Week 8 Assessment**

Find a pattern to help you solve the problem.

Bryan made a game by creating a pattern with square cards. To win, his sister had to figure out how to continue the pattern. What did Bryan do to make each new group? How many cards should his sister put in the next group?

□   □□   ▥   ▥▥   ▦

Show Your Work   **Explain Your Work**

Restate Your Answer

Name _____ Week 9

 Strategy: Use place value.

Read the problem carefully. Use what you know about place value to help solve the problem. Then, write your complete answer.

Day 1

Kevin and Carrie were playing a game where you roll 3 number cubes and try to make the greatest number possible. Kevin rolled a 4, 5, and 2. Carrie rolled a 1, 5, and 6. Who won the round? By how many points?

Day 2

Mr. Ito needed 5 items at the hardware store. He had $100 to spend. The prices of the items are listed below. Round the cost of each item to estimate if he has enough money.

hammer: $18; saw: $32; paint: $27; nails: $4; measuring tape: $9

Day 3

The theater sold 529 tickets to a show for Friday night and estimated they would sell 60 more tickets for the Saturday night show. About how many hundreds of tickets does the theater think they will sell for the Saturday night show?

Day 4

There are 778 students at Franklin Elementary. If 119 students are in 4th grade and 104 students are in 5th grade, about how many students are in grades K–3?

CD-105011 • © Carson-Dellosa   25

Name _____   Week 9 Assessment

Use place value to help you solve the problem.

Mrs. Taylor wrote the number 631 on the board. She told Brad to add 8 to the number, then told Greta to add 50 to the number, and then told Lily to add 300 to the number. What was the new number? What complete number did they add to the original number?

Show Your Work   **Explain Your Work**

Restate Your Answer

Name _____ Week 10

 Strategy: Use a bar model with parts of a whole.

Read the problem carefully. Create a bar model to show how the parts make a whole. In a problem, sometimes the whole is unknown and sometimes a part is unknown. Then, solve the problem and write your complete answer.

Part	Part

Whole

Day 1

Preston scored 18 points in the first half of the basketball game and 27 points in the second half of the game. What was his point total for the whole game?

Day 2

A clothing company had 250 shirts to dye. They dyed 160 of the shirts blue and the rest red. How many shirts were red?

Day 3

Anya gets 45 minutes to play on her tablet each day. If she played for 28 minutes before dinner, how many minutes does she have left to play after dinner?

Day 4

Duncan goes to the post office to buy stamps. He buys two 42-cent stamps and one 27-cent stamp. How much did he spend?

Name _____　　　　**Week 10 Assessment**

Use a bar model to help you solve the problem.

There were 94 third graders on a field trip at the museum. One tour guide took 45 students and a second tour guide took the rest. How many students were in the second tour group?

Show Your Work

Explain Your Work

Restate Your Answer

Name _____   Week 11

Strategy: Use a bar model for comparison.

Read the problem carefully. Create a bar model to compare two amounts. Then, solve the problem and write your complete answer.

Difference

Day 1

Kristina's mom is 35 years old and her dad is 42. How much older is Kristina's dad than her mom?

Day 2

There are two elementary schools in Bella's neighborhood. There are 592 students at her school and 403 students at the other school. How many more students go to Bella's school than the other school?

Day 3

Don has 84 more stamps in his collection than Sue. Sue has 59 stamps. How many stamps does Don have?

Day 4

Two third-grade classes collected 700 soup can labels. Maria's class collected 100 more labels than Seth's class. How many labels did Maria's class and Seth's class each collect?

Name _____

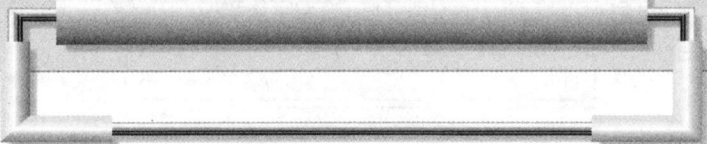

Use a bar model to help you solve the problem.

An amusement park counted 790 people who rode the Big Coaster on Saturday and 137 fewer people who rode that same ride on Sunday. How many people rode the Big Coaster on Sunday?

Show Your Work

Explain Your Work

Restate Your Answer

Name _____

Week 12

 Strategy: Act it out.

Read the problem carefully. Use objects to act out the problem. Then, solve and write your complete answer.

Day 1

Misha is making fruit baskets for gifts. He wants to put 4 pears in each basket. If he makes 5 fruit baskets, how many pears will he need?

Day 2

Pencils come in boxes of 8. If Kiki buys 2 boxes, how many pencils will she have?

Day 3

Tanner has 6 rabbit cages. Each cage has 3 rabbits. How many rabbits does Tanner have altogether?

Day 4

Ling has 4 bags of marbles. Each bag has 9 marbles in it. How many marbles does Ling have?

Name _____ **Week 12 Assessment**

Act it out to help you solve the problem.

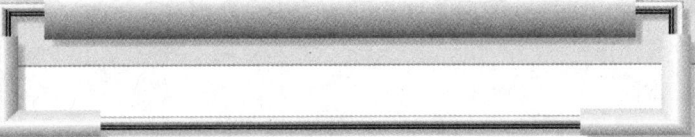

Ms. Harvey put her students into teams of 5 for the Math Bowl. There are 5 full teams and one team of 4. How many students are in Ms. Harvey's class?

Show Your Work

Explain Your Work

Restate Your Answer

Name _____ Week 13

 **Strategy: Draw a picture.**

Read the problem carefully. Draw a picture of the problem. Then, solve and write your complete answer.

Day 1

There are 4 rows of desks in Mr. Cross's third grade class. Each row has 7 desks. How many desks are in Mr. Cross's class?

Day 2

Olivia organized her shoes in a shoe cabinet that was 8 sections across and 6 sections tall. How many pairs of shoes could Olivia store in her shoe cabinet?

Day 3

Mrs. Hart arranged some grammar posters on her wall in an arrangement of 3 rows of 4 posters. How many posters did Mrs. Hart put on the wall?

Day 4

Frank arranged his baseball trading cards in a frame. The frame fits 6 cards across and 3 cards down. How many trading cards can Frank put in the frame?

Name _____ **Week 13 Assessment**

Draw a picture to help you solve the problem.

Briana is putting foam tiles on her playroom floor. She finds that 5 tiles fit along the width of the room and 7 tiles fit along the length of the room. How many foam tiles does Briana need to cover her floor completely?

Show Your Work

Explain Your Work

Restate Your Answer

Name _____   Week 14

 Strategy: Write a number sentence.

Read the problem carefully. Write a number sentence for the problem. Then, solve and write your complete answer.

Day 1

Erica brought a new box of 24 crayons to school. Her partner already had 18 crayons. How many crayons did they have together?

Day 2

The soccer coach at West High School organizes all of his players into 9 teams for a practice session on the field. Each team has 6 players. How many players are practicing on the field?

Day 3

Kim bought a set of 18 new plates. When she put them in the dishwasher, 4 of them broke. She got 6 new ones as a gift. How many plates does Kim have now?

Day 4

Mrs. Walsh has 6 rows ready to plant in her garden. She wants to plant 7 pepper plants in each row of her garden. She also has a pot on her porch with 3 pepper plants. How many pepper plants will she have in all?

Name _____  Week 14 Assessment

Write a number sentence to help you solve the problem.

Mateo is cooking a dish to bring to a potluck dinner at his adventurers' club meeting. The recipe calls for 32 meatballs. The instructions on the bag of meatballs say to cook 2 minutes for every 8 meatballs. How long does Mateo need to cook the meatballs?

Show Your Work

Explain Your Work

Restate Your Answer

Name _____   Week 15

 Strategy: Use a symbol for the unknown.

Read the problem carefully. Write a multiplication number sentence and use a symbol for the unknown quantity. Then, solve and write your complete answer.

Day 1

Josie is decorating 3 shirts for her friends. She wants each shirt to have the same number of buttons. If she uses 27 buttons to decorate the shirts, how many buttons are on each shirt?

Day 2

A party planner was arranging chairs around 9 tables for a party. She put the same amount of chairs at each table. If there will be 72 guests, how many chairs did she put at each table?

Day 3

Payton shared her stickers equally between herself and her 5 friends. If she had a sheet of 48 stickers, how many stickers did Payton and her friends each get?

Day 4

The tennis coach gave each of his 4 students the same number of practice balls. If he had a total of 32 tennis balls, how many did he give to each student?

Name _____

Week 15 Assessment

Write a symbol for the unknown amount to help you solve the problem.

Faith bought a super saver box of dog bones. There were 4 bags of bones in the box, and the box said there were 80 bones total in the box. If Faith gave one of the bags to a friend, how many dog bones did she give away?

Show Your Work

Explain Your Work

Restate Your Answer

Name _____

Week 16

 **Strategy: Restate the problem in your own words.**

Read the problem carefully. Restate the problem in your own words to help you understand the question. Then, solve and write your complete answer.

Day 1

Zoe has saved $20 to buy a fish tank and some fish. She bought a tank for $12, and the fish will cost $2 each. How many fish can she buy?

Day 2

Karen was making 8 goody bags for her birthday party. She has 64 stickers. She decorates each bag with 3 stickers. How many stickers does she have left to put in each goody bag?

Day 3

Alejandra writes 3 pages in her journal each day. How many pages does she write in a week?

Day 4

Ian's service club meets twice a week. At each meeting, they plan 3 service projects. How many service projects will Ian's club plan in a month?

Name _____

Week 16 Assessment

Restate the problem in your own words to help you solve the problem.

Noah's mother told him she would pay him $5 an hour to babysit his little brother. Noah babysat for 3 hours Monday, 3 hours on Wednesday, and 4 hours on Friday. How much money did Noah make for babysitting in all?

Show Your Work

Explain Your Work

Restate Your Answer

Name _____   Week 17

 Strategy: Guess and check.

Read the problem carefully. Use estimation to make a guess that makes sense. Then, solve to check your guess. Write your complete answer.

Day 1

Travis has $3.00 to spend at the ice-cream shop. A single scoop costs $2.39, and extra sprinkles cost $0.99. Does Travis have enough money to get extra sprinkles?

Day 2

Melissa wants to make bookmarks for each of her 5 friends. She needs 6 inches of paper for each one. She has 28 inches of bookmark paper. Will she be able to make a bookmark for each friend?

Day 3

Joe's aunt baked 4 dozen cookies for his class's end-of-year picnic. There are 21 students in his class. Will there be enough so that every student can have 2 cookies each?

Day 4

Lucinda has 18 pansies, 12 geraniums, and 6 marigolds. If Lucinda has 3 pots, will she be able to plant the same number of each type of flowers in each pot?

Name _____   **Week 17 Assessment**

Guess and check to help you solve the problem.

In Mr. Kay's music class, there are 10 students. There are 6 more girls than boys. How many boys are in the music class? How many girls are in the class?

Show Your Work

Explain Your Work

Restate Your Answer

Name _____ Week 18

 Strategy: Use the CUBES strategy.

Read the problem carefully. **C**ircle the important numbers. **U**nderline the question. **B**ox the key words. **E**liminate extra information. **S**olve and check your answer.

Day 1

John is riding the bus to his grandparents' house. There are 79 people waiting for buses. While John buys his ticket, 24 people get on the bus he is taking. If the bus can seat 50 passengers, how many more people can get on the bus?

Day 2

A toy factory manager sets a goal of making 750 toys by December. The factory's workers can make 90 toys a day. After 5 days, the workers have made 450 toys. How many more toys do they need to make to reach the manager's goal?

Day 3

Ariel is in a 200-meter relay race. Each team has 4 runners. Ariel runs the first 50 meters and hands the baton to her teammate. Her teammate runs the next 50 meters. The third teammate also runs 50 meters when the baton is handed to her. How many meters will the last runner have to run to complete the race?

Day 4

The mail carrier works an 8-hour day. She delivers letters to 10 houses on a city block. She delivers 4 letters to each house. How many letters in all does the mail carrier deliver on that one city block?

Name _____

Week 18 Assessment

Use the CUBES strategy to help you solve the problem.

Shawn and his friends are planting tomatoes in a community garden. Shawn plants 5 rows of 4 tomato seedlings. One friend plants 2 rows of 4 seedlings, and another friend plants 9 rows of 6 seedlings. How many tomato seedlings do Shawn and his friends plant altogether in the garden?

Show Your Work

Explain Your Work

Restate Your Answer

Name _____ Week 19

 Strategy: Solve a simpler problem.

Read the problem carefully. Solve a related, simpler problem first and use it to solve the actual problem. Write your complete answer.

Day 1

Adam and his dad are on the way to the beach. The beach is 420 miles away. If they drive at 60 miles an hour, how many hours should it take to drive there?

Day 2

Ms. Willis is fixing ham biscuits for a party and needs 4 pounds of ham. Deli ham costs $3.50 a pound. How much will Ms. Willis pay for 4 pounds of ham?

Day 3

Luke's whole school went on a field trip to the zoo. There were 560 students, and 70 students can go on each school bus. How many school buses did the principal need to have for the trip?

Day 4

Tamara was training for a marathon. She ran 15 miles a day for 2 months (60 days) before the race. How many miles did she run in all?

Name _____

Week 19 Assessment

Solve a simpler problem to help you solve the problem.

Three friends have a total of $10 to spend on snacks at the movies. They each want popcorn, which costs $3.18 a bag. Do they have enough money? If so, how much is left over?

Show Your Work

Explain Your Work

Restate Your Answer

Name _____   Week 20

 Strategy: Act it out.

Read the problem carefully. Use objects to act out the problem. Then, solve and write your complete answer.

Day 1

There are 24 new car tires at the car shop. How many cars can get a full set of new tires from the shop?

Day 2

Nolan has 32 mice and 4 cages. If he wants to put an equal number of mice in each cage, how many mice will be in each cage?

Day 3

Eric is paper-clipping packets of papers for school. He has 48 papers and he must put 6 papers in each packet. How many paper clips will Eric need?

Day 4

Holly had 21 hair bows. She gave some friends 3 each of her hair bows. How many friends did Holly give hair bows to?

Name _____   Week 20 Assessment

Act it out to help you solve the problem.

A zoo has 23 amphibians to put in 4 new habitats. Eight of them need to go together and the rest can be divided evenly between the other habitats. How many amphibians will be in each of the other habitats?

Show Your Work

Explain Your Work

Restate Your Answer

Name _____ Week 21

 Strategy: Write a number sentence.

Read the problem carefully. Write a number sentence for the problem. Then, solve and write your complete answer.

Day 1

Mr. Daniels asked Bo and Gia to divide the 54 class markers into 6 buckets, one for each student table. How many markers did each table get?

Day 2

Mara baked 56 cookies. She has 7 friends she wants to evenly give the cookies to. How many cookies will each friend get?

Day 3

Hector tackled a total of 36 football players in the last 4 games. He tackled the same number of players each game. How many players did Hector tackle each game?

Day 4

Lisa volunteers at the hospital. She worked a total of 40 hours in March. She worked for the same number of hours each day that she volunteered. If she volunteered a total of 8 days in March, how many hours did she work each day?

CD-105011 • © Carson-Dellosa

49

Name _____

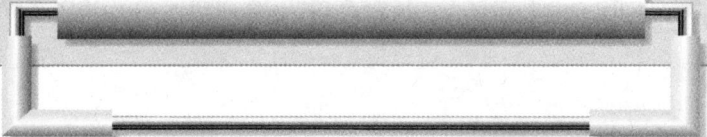

Write a number sentence to help you solve the problem.

The pet store got in a new shipment of 45 goldfish. The pet store manager wants to be sure the fish aren't too crowded in one tank, so he tells the employees to divide the fish evenly between the five empty fish tanks. How many fish should the employees put in each tank?

Show Your Work

Explain Your Work

Restate Your Answer

Name _____ Week 22

 Strategy: Use logical reasoning.

Read the problem carefully. Use logical reasoning to solve. Then, write your complete answer.

Day 1

Tracy forgot her homework at school. She knows she was supposed to find the difference between two odd 3-digit numbers under 500. She also knows the answer to the problem is 122. What could Tracy's homework problem be?

Day 2

Grant picked a number between 20 and 50. He gives his friends some hints about the number. He says the number is even, and the smaller digit is in the tens place. He says you can multiply 6 by another number to get his number, and you get 6 if you add the 2 digits of the number together. What number did Grant pick?

Day 3

Priya has 75 marbles in her collection. Tyler has 23 fewer marbles than Priya, and Julie has 38 more marbles than Tyler. How many marbles does Julie have?

Day 4

Sophia is 7 years older than Ansley. Their ages add up to 21. How old are Sophia and Ansley?

Name _____   **Week 22 Assessment**

Use logical reasoning to help you solve the problem.

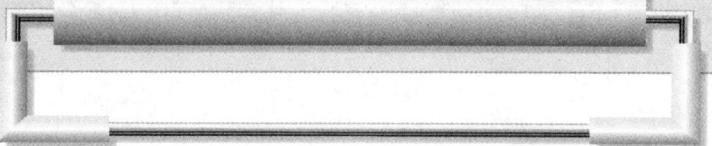

Randy has 200 trading cards. Over the years, his parents gave him some, his friends gave him some, and he bought some. Randy's parents gave him twice as many trading cards as his friends did. He got an equal amount from his friends and his own purchases. How many cards did Randy get from his parents?

Show Your Work

Explain Your Work

Restate Your Answer

Name _____ Week 23

 Strategy: Work backward.

Read the problem carefully. Work backward to solve. Then, write your complete answer.

Day 1

Zoe and her mom made some cupcakes on Saturday. Zoe's brother ate 2 of the cupcakes. On Sunday, Zoe's mom took 14 of the cupcakes to her sewing group, and that night each of Zoe's four family members ate one cupcake. There were 4 cupcakes left for Zoe to give to her friends. How many cupcakes did Zoe and her mom make?

Day 2

Paul thought of a number. He added 4 to it and multiplied the result by 2. Then, he subtracted 4 and divided by 7. The number Paul ended up with was 2. What was Paul's original number?

Day 3

Anita got her paycheck on Friday. She paid her friend $10 that she owed her. Then, she spent half of her check on some new clothes. She bought a treat at the bakery for $4 and now she has $6 left. How much was Anita's paycheck?

Day 4

Mark set his alarm early for a track meet that starts at 8:00 a.m. He hit the snooze button twice for 8 minutes more sleep each time. It will take him 20 minutes to get ready and 9 minutes to get to the meet. If he gets there 5 minutes before the meet begins, what time did he set his alarm clock for?

Name _____   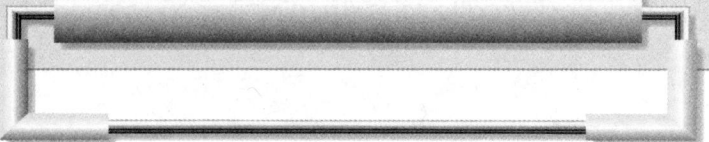 **Week 23 Assessment**

Work backward to help you solve the problem.

Amy baked some brownies on Saturday. Amy's brother ate 1 of them while they were still warm. Her dad ate 3 of them when he got home. Her mother didn't want any and gave 8 of them to their neighbors. By dinnertime, there were only 4 left. How many brownies had Amy baked to start with?

Show Your Work

Explain Your Work

Restate Your Answer

Name _____   Week 24

 Strategy: Make an organized list.

Read the problem carefully. Make an organized list to help you solve the problem. Then, write your complete answer.

Day 1

Jocelyn found some starfish. Each starfish had 5 arms. Jocelyn's brother found some crabs. Each crab had 8 legs. If all the animals they found had 49 arms and legs altogether, how many starfish and crabs did Jocelyn and her brother find?

Day 2

Joe, Yuan, Drake, and Ace are in computer club. They are having their picture taken for the yearbook and can't decide in what order they should line up. What are all of the different ways they could line up for their photo? How many different options are there?

Day 3

Rhett has to wear a uniform to school each day. He can wear black or khaki pants that can be either shorts or long pants. He can also wear a white or red polo shirt that can either be short-sleeve or long-sleeve. How many different outfits does Rhett have to wear to school?

Day 4

Walt's art club painted pictures for a local hospital. They could each paint a landscape, a portrait, a still life, or an abstract painting. They could also place their pictures in the ER, the nursery, or the family waiting room. Their pictures could have a white frame or a black frame. How many different options does Walt have for his painting?

Name _____

Week 24 Assessment

Make an organized list to help you solve the problem.

Mr. Evans got a new digital door lock system. The system picked an entry code at random using the digits he chose: 3, 5, and 7. Mr. Evans can't remember the code. What are all of the possible combinations he should try?

Show Your Work

Explain Your Work

Restate Your Answer

Name _____   Week 25

 Strategy: Make a table.

Read the problem carefully. Make a table to help you solve the problem. Then, write your complete answer.

Day 1

Mr. Carson needs to order 80 textbooks for the new school year. The books come in boxes of 16. How many boxes will he need to order?

Day 2

Sasha has a pack of 24 lemon-lime candies. For every yellow candy, the pack has 3 green candies. How many yellow candies and green candies are in the pack?

Day 3

Connor has $500 in his bank account. Every month, $35 is taken out to pay for his gym membership. Does he have enough money to pay for a year of gym membership?

Day 4

Becca likes collecting stickers. Her favorite brand comes in packs of 5 sheets. Each sticker sheet has 8 stickers on it. How many stickers will she have if she buys 6 packs?

Name _____

Week 25 Assessment

Make a table to help you solve the problem.

Every Wednesday, Bobby's Bagels has a buy-two-get-one-free sale. If Graham's mom needs to bring 2 dozen bagels for the teacher appreciation breakfast, how many bagels will she need to buy?

Show Your Work

Explain Your Work

Restate Your Answer

Name _____   Week 26

 Strategy: Break the problem into smaller parts.

Read the problem carefully. Break the problem into smaller parts to solve. Then, write your complete answer.

Day 1

The gym where Amy takes gymnastics put in new floor mats. Look at the measurements of the mats. What is the total area?

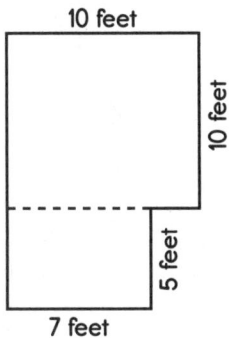

Day 2

Oscar is putting down sod in his backyard. The yard is a rectangle that is 8 yards by 9 yards and has 2 smaller squares on each side that are 5 yards on each side. How many square yards of sod does Oscar need to order?

Day 3

Isabel's family is putting new tile in the kitchen, but not in the closet. Look at the floor plan. How much tile will Isabel's family need?

☐ = square foot

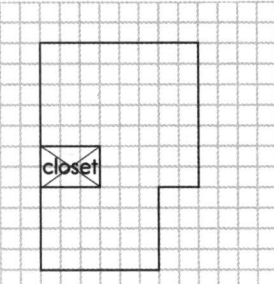

Day 4

Nathan was making a paper project for art class. He knew he needed 2 rectangles that were each 30 centimeters by 40 centimeters and 2 rectangles that were each 50 centimeters by 50 centimeters. How much paper will Nathan need?

Name _____   Week 26 Assessment

Break the problem into smaller parts to help you solve the problem.

Cara has a closet shaped like the figure shown. She wants to put down carpet tiles that cost $3 per square foot. How much money will she have to spend?

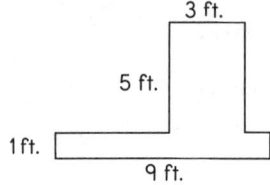

Show Your Work | **Explain Your Work**

Restate Your Answer

Name _____

Week 27

 Strategy: Draw a picture.

Read the problem carefully. Draw a picture to help you solve the problem. Then, write your complete answer.

Day 1

Rachel completed $\frac{3}{4}$ of her homework and Lily completed $\frac{1}{2}$ of her homework. Who completed more homework? By how much?

Day 2

Stefan's mom cut four pans of brownies and gave away half of each pan. She cut the first pan into 2 pieces, the second pan into 4 pieces, the third pan into 12 pieces, and the fourth pan into 8 pieces. How many pieces of brownie did Stefan's mom give away?

Day 3

Chris's dad said he could eat $\frac{1}{2}$ of a candy bar or $\frac{5}{8}$ of a candy bar. Which option should Chris take if he wanted more candy?

Day 4

Each of two cakes were cut into 6 slices. The bake shop sold $1\frac{2}{3}$ cakes during the day. How many slices of cake did the bake shop sell?

Name _____   Week 27 Assessment

Draw a picture to help you solve the problem.

At lunch, Jaylen ate $\frac{1}{3}$ of a ham sandwich. Grace ate $\frac{2}{6}$ of a turkey sandwich. Did they both eat the same amount of their sandwiches? Why or why not?

Show Your Work

Explain Your Work

Restate Your Answer

Name _____ Week 28

 Strategy: Use a number line.

Read the problem carefully. Use a number line to show fractions and help you solve the problem. Then, write your complete answer. The problem for Day 1 has been started for you.

Day 1

Darla ate $\frac{1}{2}$ of an orange. Xavier ate $\frac{4}{6}$ of an orange. Who ate more of their orange?

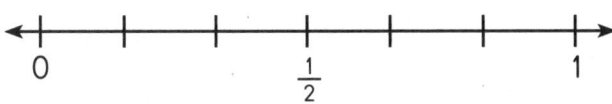

Day 2

Rosa's mom spends $\frac{2}{8}$ of her time at work in meetings and spends the rest of the time on the sales floor. How much of her time at work does she spend on the sales floor?

Day 3

Nancy makes punch that is $\frac{2}{5}$ pineapple juice and the rest orange juice. What fraction of the punch is orange juice?

Day 4

Tia won a large candy bar as a prize at the fair. She wanted to share it with her 5 friends, but she didn't know how to divide it evenly. How much of the candy bar should each friend get?

Name _____

Week 28 Assessment

Draw a number line to help you solve the problem.

Ashley has $\frac{2}{6}$ of an apple pie left over from the family picnic. She wants to trade her cousin for some of her blueberry pie. The blueberry pie is cut into 12 slices. She wants to trade the same amount of pie to be fair. How many pieces of blueberry pie should Ashley get for the rest of her apple pie?

Show Your Work

Explain Your Work

Restate Your Answer

Name _____ Week 29

 Strategy: Use a bar model with equal parts.

Read the problem carefully. Use a bar model to show the equal parts of the whole and help you solve the problem. For example, the bar model below can help you solve Day 1. Then, write your complete answer.

Part
[bar model with 4 equal sections]
Whole

Day 1

Mrs. Sweeney bought a long, rectangular bar of homemade soap at the craft fair. She cut it into equal sections to put in each of the 4 bathrooms in her house. If the soap bar was advertised as lasting for 200 hand-washings, how many hand-washings can she expect to get from each of the sections?

Day 2

Erik bought a long submarine sandwich that was cut into 6 equal serving sizes. The sub shop listed the calories for one serving size as 115 calories. How many calories was the entire submarine sandwich?

Day 3

Hayley is painting a banner for the school football team to run through at the start of the first game of the season. She wants to paint the letters of the team name—PANTHERS—evenly spaced across the banner. The paper she is painting is 8 yards long. How many feet long will each letter space be?

Day 4

Lukas has listened to 5 of the 12 songs on his favorite band's new album. Each song on the album is 2 minutes long. For how much longer must he listen to music to hear all of the songs?

CD-105011 • © Carson-Dellosa   65

Name _____

Week 29 Assessment

Use a bar model to help you solve the problem.

Tiffany has a lot of math problems to solve for homework. She decides to divide the work into 5 problem groups. She times herself as she works on the first group and finds that it takes her 28 minutes to finish $\frac{1}{5}$ of the problems. How long should she estimate it will take her to finish all her homework?

Show Your Work

Explain Your Work

Restate Your Answer

Name _____   Week 30

 Strategy: Use a conversion chart.

Read the problem carefully. Use the conversion chart to help you solve the problem. Then, write your complete answer.

| 1 quart (qt.) = 4 cups (c.) |
| 1 gallon (gal.) = 4 quarts (qt.) |
| 1 gallon (gal.) = 8 pints (pt.) |
| 1 gallon (gal.) = 16 cups (c.) |

Day 1

Mr. McCoy buys 3 quarts of apple cider for a party. There will be 11 people at the party. Will he have enough to serve each guest one cup of apple cider?

Day 2

Ms. Perez buys 2 gallons of lemonade for her son's birthday party. Will she have enough lemonade to serve each of her 20 guests two cups?

Day 3

Mr. Stone read an article that said it was healthy to drink 2 quarts of water a day. His water bottle only measures in cups. How many cups of water should Mr. Stone drink each day?

Day 4

Mrs. Gant buys 5 gallons of ice cream. She wants to fill 40 pint containers with the ice cream to sell at a carnival. Did she buy enough ice cream?

Name _____   **Week 30 Assessment**

Use a conversion chart to help you solve the problem.

Kedra needs to buy 7 yards of blue fabric to make new curtains. How many feet of blue fabric will she buy?

| 1 foot (ft.) = 12 inches (in.) |
| 1 yard (yd.) = 3 feet (ft.) |
| 1 yard (yd.) = 36 inches (in.) |

Show Your Work | **Explain Your Work**

Restate Your Answer

Name _____   Week 31

 Strategy: Use a formula.

Read the problem carefully. Use the formulas for perimeter and area to help you solve the problem. Then, write your complete answer.

Perimeter = (2 × length) + (2 × width)   Area = length × width

Day 1

Kodi and his dad were building a fence around their backyard. If their yard is 15 feet long and 10 feet wide, how many feet of fencing do they need to buy?

Day 2

Fatima wants to cover her sister's bedroom door with wrapping paper as a birthday surprise. The door is 7 feet tall and 3 feet wide. If she buys 24 square feet of wrapping paper, will she have enough to cover the door?

Day 3

Yolanda and her grandmother made a quilt that is 8 feet long and 6 feet wide. Yolanda wants to sew a trim around the edges of the quilt. How long of a piece of trim should Yolanda's grandmother buy?

Day 4

Jack built a sandbox in his backyard. The sandbox was 2 meters wide and the area was 6 square meters. How long was the sandbox?

Name _____   **Week 31 Assessment**

Use a formula to help you solve the problem.

A handyman is repairing 2 glass windows. The first window measures 9 inches by 7 inches. The second window measures 8 inches by 4 inches. He has 125 square inches of glass. Does he have enough glass left to replace a third 8-inch by 4-inch window?

Show Your Work

Explain Your Work

Restate Your Answer

Name _____ Week 32

 Strategy: Draw a diagram.

Read the problem carefully. Draw a diagram to help you solve the problem. Then, write your complete answer.

Day 1

Wren is decorating the top of a box that is 2 inches long by 3 inches wide. She wants to cover the top of the box lid completely with patterned paper. How many square inches of paper will she need?

Day 2

Jenn is stuck on a geometry problem. She is supposed to partition a hexagon into six equal parts. She doesn't think it can be done. What should her solution look like?

Day 3

Landon is planting a rectangular garden that is 20 feet long by 5 feet wide. He wants to plant at least 20 square feet of sunflowers, 50 square feet of lilies, and 30 square feet of daisies. How could Landon divide his garden?

Day 4

Sam ate 3 slices of a pizza that was cut into 12 equal slices. Michelle ate 2 slices of a same size pizza cut into 8 equal slices. Who ate more pizza?

Name _____   Week 32 Assessment

Draw a diagram to help you solve the problem.

Brent is building a dog pen in his yard. His yard measures 10 meters by 10 meters. The area of the dog pen needs to be greater than 20 square meters and Brent wants at least 70 square meters of the yard to be unfenced. What could be the length and width of the largest dog pen Brent can make?

Show Your Work

Explain Your Work

Restate Your Answer

Name _____

Week 33

 Strategy: Use a number line.

Read the problem carefully. Use a number line to help you solve the problem. For example, the number line below can help you solve the problem for Day 1. Then, write your complete answer.

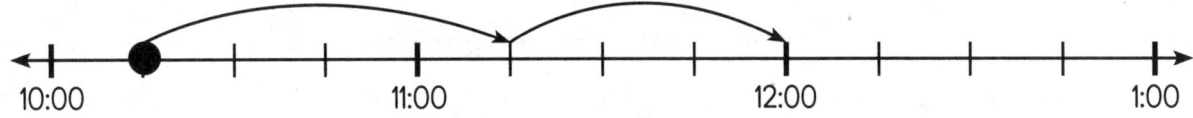

Day 1

Mr. Garcia met with the school board at 10:15. His meeting lasted for 1 hour and 45 minutes. What time was the meeting over?

Day 2

Cade knows it takes him 5 minutes to complete each part of his bedtime routine. He always washes his face, brushes his teeth, puts on his pajamas, and says goodnight to his parents. His bedtime is 8:30. What time does Cade need to start getting ready for bed?

Day 3

Raul is supposed to read each day for at least 40 minutes. He read from 4:25 until 5:15. Did he read enough for the day? For how many minutes did he read?

Day 4

Elise wants to meet her friends at the movie theater on Friday. The movie starts at 6:20. She has a piano lesson at 4:45. Her lesson lasts for 45 minutes. It takes 35 minutes for her mom to drive her from the piano lesson to the movie theater. Will she make it to the movies on time?

Name _____   **Week 33 Assessment**

Draw a number line to help you solve the problem.

Cindy practiced the piano from 3:15 to 3:45 on Monday and from 3:30 until 4:00 on Tuesday. Cindy needs to practice for $1\frac{1}{2}$ hours total before her piano lesson on Thursday. If she starts practicing at 3:00 on Wednesday, what time can she stop so she has practiced enough time before her lesson?

Show Your Work | **Explain Your Work**

Restate Your Answer

Name _____ Week 34

 Strategy: Use estimation.

Read the problem carefully. Use estimation to help you solve the problem without doing the exact computation. Then, write your complete answer.

Day 1

Natalie has $50 to spend on some new clothes. She decides to buy a dress that cost $24.79, a T-shirt that cost $9.25, and some shorts that cost $12.50. At the register, she sees some earrings she likes for $1.99. Will she have enough money to buy the earrings? Why or why not?

Day 2

Henry is invited to go skating with his friends at 2:30 p.m. He has a soccer game at 10:30 a.m. The game lasts for 57 minutes, and he drives for 25 minutes to the store. He spends 1 hour and 22 minutes at the store. It takes 45 minutes to get to the skating rink from the store. Can Henry get to the rink in time? How do you know?

Day 3

Maggie's family is visiting the aquarium. Her parents give Maggie and her brother $8 each to buy items at the gift shop. Maggie wants a stuffed penguin for $7.49 and her brother wants a toy stingray for $5.35. They also want to share a sea animal sticker pack that costs $2.99. If they combine their money, can they buy all the items they want?

Day 4

Doug works at the checkout counter at the grocery store. Ms. Rogers paid for $84.13 worth of groceries with a one-hundred-dollar bill. Doug says he doesn't have any twenty-dollar bills in his register, so he'll have to give her 2 ten-dollar bills with her change. Ms. Rogers says that's too much change. Who is right? About how much change should she get?

Name _____   **Week 34 Assessment**

Estimate to help you solve the problem.

The school secretary has a budget of $100 to buy office supplies. On her list are 2 boxes of copy paper for a total of $44.67 and a power pencil sharpener for $33.99. She also needs a box of tape rolls for $18.20 and a new calculator for $24.78, but she thinks she only has money to buy one of those. Which does she have enough money in the budget to buy, the box of tape rolls or the calculator?

Show Your Work

Explain Your Work

Restate Your Answer

Name _____   Week 35

 Strategy: Use a symbol for the unknown.

Read the problem carefully. Write an equation and use a symbol for the unknown to help you solve the problem. Then, write your complete answer.

Day 1

A baker has 300 grams of sugar. He uses some to bake a cake. Now he has 154 grams of sugar left. How much sugar did the baker use in the cake?

Day 2

Kelly wanted to weigh her cat, but she couldn't get her to sit still on the scale. So, she held her cat and weighed herself and the cat together. Kelly knows she weighs 36 kilograms and together they weighed 42 kilograms. How much does Kelly's cat weigh?

Day 3

A full fish tank weighs 160 pounds. Aaron removes 5 gallons to clean the tank. Now the fish tank weighs 120 pounds. How much does 1 gallon of water weigh?

Day 4

Mr. Brown's neighbor gave him a load of mulch. He used 430 pounds of it in his flower beds and he had 170 pounds left. How many pounds of mulch were originally in the load of mulch given to Mr. Brown?

Name _____

Week 35 Assessment

Write an equation and use a symbol for the unknown to help you solve the problem.

A cider mill had some apples for making cider. Each gallon of cider takes 20 pounds of apples. They made 24 gallons of cider from the apples. How many pounds of apples did they press to make the cider?

Show Your Work

Explain Your Work

Restate Your Answer

Name _____   Week 36

 Strategy: Use a logic grid.

Read the problem carefully. Create a grid with items from one category across the top and items from another category along the left side. Draw a check mark or an X in each block to help you solve the problem. Then, write your complete answer. Day 1 has been started for you.

Day 1

Three friends (Sara, Morgan, Tina) went to the fair, and they each won a prize (a fish, sunglasses, a teddy bear). Sarah didn't get the fish. No friend got a prize that starts with the same letter as her name. Morgan can wear her prize. Who won each prize?

	Fish	Sunglasses	Teddy Bear
Sara			
Morgan			
Tina			

Day 2

Tyrone and his sisters, Tia and Tanya, are each eating a different fruit (apple, banana, orange). Tia doesn't have to peel her fruit. Tyrone's fruit is juicy. Who ate which fruit?

Day 3

Four students (Erin, Hank, Ray, and Nina) are in the lunch line at school. Nina is not first or last. Ray is behind Hank, and no one is behind Ray. Who is first in line?

Day 4

Luis bought his 4 pets (dog, bird, cat, bunny) each a gift (bell, ball, treat, dish). The dog didn't get a gift that starts with a *b*. The cat and the bird each got something to play with. The cat and dog did not get something to eat. The bird liked to make noise with his gift. Which pet got which gift?

Name _____

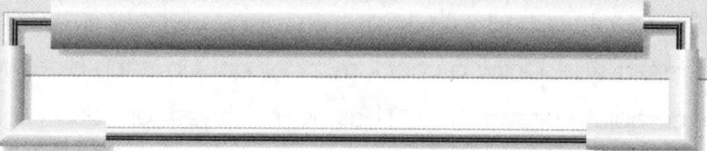

Week 36 Assessment

Use a logic grid to help you solve the problem.

A delivery driver had different shaped packages (cube, sphere, cylinder, pyramid) to deliver to different colored houses (red, blue, green, and yellow). The package that went to the red house did not have any flat faces. The pyramid package did not go to the yellow house. The package that went to the green house had the most flat faces, and they were all the same size. Which houses did the packages get delivered to?

Show Your Work	Explain Your Work

Restate Your Answer

Name _____ Week 37

 Strategy: Draw a picture.

Read the problem carefully. Draw a picture to help you solve the problem. Then, write your complete answer.

Day 1

Mr. Wendell wanted a new garden. He had 12 meters of new fencing for his garden, but he didn't want just a rectangle shape. Design 4 different garden shapes with a perimeter of 12 meters for Mr. Wendell to choose from.

Day 2

Kate wanted to build a pen for her rabbit. She wants a pen to have an area of 8 square feet and have the greatest perimeter possible. She used 8 squares to try making different plans. How should she design her rabbit pen?

Day 3

Maria has to build a fence around her backyard to keep her dogs in. Her backyard measures 16 yards by 8 yards. She will need to place fence posts every 4 yards to hold the fencing. How much fencing will Maria need? How many fence posts will Maria need to purchase?

Day 4

Pete's grandmother is making a quilt from Pete's old T-shirts. She has enough fabric to make 16 one-foot squares. She wants the trim around the border to have the same perimeter as the area of the quilt. How should she arrange the quilt squares?

Name _____   **Week 37 Assessment**

Draw a picture to help you solve the problem.

Caleb is making a 3-foot wide path all around his garden. The garden inside the path is a square and has an area of 36 square feet. What will be the perimeter of his garden after he adds the path?

Show Your Work

Explain Your Work

Restate Your Answer

Name _____ Week 38

 Strategy: Make a list and eliminate.

Read the problem carefully. Make a list of possible answers based on some information, then eliminate choices based on more information from the problem. Then, write your complete answer.

Day 1

Kylie picked two numbers that had a sum of 18 and a difference of 8. What were Kylie's numbers?

Day 2

Rhonda picked a number whose digits had a product of 16 and difference of 6. What was Rhonda's number?

Day 3

Sadie asked Rick a riddle: What two 1-digit numbers have a 1-digit product, but a 2-digit sum?

Day 4

Jeff drew two shapes and gave his sister two clues about which shapes he drew. He told her that together, his shapes have 11 sides and one shape has 5 more sides than the other shape. What two shapes did Jeff draw?

Name _____

Week 38 Assessment

Write a list and eliminate choices to help you solve the problem.

Dana was picking out boxes for the bracelets she makes. She needed boxes that had an area of 36 square centimeters, but she also needed the boxes to be over twice as long as they are wide. What could be the length and width of the boxes?

Show Your Work

Explain Your Work

Restate Your Answer

Name _____

Week 39

 **Strategy: Use equivalent fractions.**

Read the problem carefully. Use equivalent fractions to help you solve the problem. Then, write your complete answer.

Day 1

Frank cut a pie into 6 equal slices. He ate 3 slices and left the rest for Jo. Is this fair? How do you know?

Day 2

Parker's dad made a pizza for lunch and told Parker he could either have $\frac{2}{6}$ or $\frac{1}{3}$ of the pizza. Parker picked $\frac{2}{6}$ because 2 is more than 1. Is it more? Why or why not?

Day 3

Shana and Amy were given the same size graham crackers for snack. Shana ate 4 pieces of her graham cracker and Amy ate 2 pieces of hers. Neither of them had any graham cracker left. How is that possible?

Day 4

Trevor ate $\frac{14}{4}$ candy bars. How many whole candy bars did he eat? How much of a candy bar was left over?

Name _____ **Week 39 Assessment**

Use equivalent fractions to help you solve the problem.

Dylan cut his apple into 8 pieces and ate 4 pieces. Oscar cut his apple into 4 pieces and ate 2 pieces. Oscar says he has more apple left than Dylan because he only ate 2 pieces and Dylan ate 4 pieces. Is he right? Explain.

Show Your Work

Explain Your Work

Restate Your Answer

Name _____   Week 40

 Strategy: Use the CUBES strategy.

Read the problem carefully. **C**ircle the important numbers. **U**nderline the question. **B**ox the key words. **E**liminate extra information. **S**olve and check your answer.

Day 1

There were 4 showings of the school play over the weekend. On Friday night, 2,156 people were in the audience. On Saturday, 1,878 people were at the noon matinee and 1,632 people were at the 7:00 show. The Sunday matinee had 949 people in the audience. Did more people come to the play on Saturday or on Friday and Sunday combined? How many more?

Day 2

A pilot flew 3 hours and 20 minutes on Friday. He flew 2 45-minute flights on Saturday. He slept for 8 hours and then flew for 1 hour and 50 minutes on Sunday. How many total hours did the pilot fly over the three days?

Day 3

A meteorologist measured the air temperature as 56° at 9:00 a.m. She observed that the temperature rose 3° every hour from 9:00 a.m. until 4:00 p.m. What was the temperature at 4 p.m?

Day 4

Mrs. True has 7 quarters and 5 dimes for bus fare. She needs to travel 6 stops before she gets off. It costs 20¢ a stop to ride the bus. Her whole trip takes about 30 minutes. How much change will Mrs. True have left when she gets off the bus, if any?

Name _____   **Week 40 Assessment**

Use the CUBES strategy to help you solve the problem.

A jeweler was making a new bracelet design for an order of 30 bracelets. He decided to use diamonds and rubies. He set 1 diamond, 1 ruby, 2 diamonds, 2 rubies, 3 diamonds, 3 rubies, and so on until he ended the bracelet with 6 rubies. If each gemstone is 4 mm long, how long will each bracelet be?

Show Your Work

Explain Your Work

Restate Your Answer

Answer Key

Page 9
Check students' work. **Day 1:** 36 balloons; **Day 2:** 57 bottles; **Day 3:** 35 more comic books; **Day 4:** 98 cans

Page 10
Check students' work and reasoning. Lauren sold 49 tickets.

Page 11
Check students' work. **Day 1:** kangaroo, by 77 pounds; **Day 2:** 89 marbles; **Day 3:** 41 glasses; **Day 4:** $99

Page 12
Check students' work and reasoning. Cameron's brother should give her 14 pennies.

Page 13
Check students' work. **Day 1:** 88 pages; **Day 2:** 44 more jellyfish; **Day 3:** 75 paper clips; **Day 4:** 37 birds

Page 14
Check students' work and reasoning. The school will have 180 math books.

Page 15
Check students' work. **Day 1:** 16 more points; **Day 2:** 95¢; **Day 3:** 83 shells; **Day 4:** $22

Page 16
Check students' work and reasoning. The team won or tied 25 games this season.

Page 17
Check students' work. **Day 1:** $143; **Day 2:** 715 scoops; **Day 3:** 425 beads; **Day 4:** $153

Page 18
Check students' work and reasoning. He needs to buy 132 more nonfiction books.

Page 19
Check students' work. **Day 1:** 11 more minutes; **Day 2:** 1,526 programs; **Day 3:** 154 in.; **Day 4:** 205 more postcards

Page 20
Check students' work and reasoning. The science club made $751.

Page 21
Check students' work. **Day 1:** grape, cranberry, and strawberry; **Day 2:** 5 more days; **Day 3:** 16 fewer votes: **Day 4:** 16 students

Page 22
Check students' work and reasoning. Sixteen more students chose the three most popular colors than the three least popular colors.

Page 23
Check students' work. **Day 1:** 10 dot stickers; **Day 2:** 18 sides; **Day 3:** 34, 44, 54, 64, 74, 84, 94; **Day 4:** 6 numbers

Page 24
Check students' work and reasoning. Bryan doubled the number of squares in each group. His sister should put 32 squares in the next group.

Page 25
Check students' work. **Day 1:** Carrie by 109 points; **Day 2:** He has enough money (about $95). **Day 3:** about 600 tickets; **Day 4:** about 560 students

Answer Key

Page 26
Check students' work and reasoning. The new number was 989 and the number added was 358.

Page 27
Check students' work. **Day 1:** 45 points;
Day 2: 90 red shirts; **Day 3:** 17 minutes; **Day 4:** $1.11

Page 28
Check students' work and reasoning. There were 49 students in the second tour group.

Page 29
Check students' work. **Day 1:** 7 years;
Day 2: 189 more students; **Day 3:** 143 stamps;
Day 4: Seth: 300 labels; Maria: 400 labels

Page 30
Check students' work and reasoning. On Sunday, 653 people rode the Big Coaster.

Page 31
Check students' work. **Day 1:** 20 pears;
Day 2: 16 pencils; **Day 3:** 18 rabbits;
Day 4: 36 marbles

Page 32
Check students' work and reasoning. There are 29 students in Ms. Harvey's class.

Page 33
Check students' work. **Day 1:** 28 desks;
Day 2: 48 pairs of shoes; **Day 3:** 12 posters;
Day 4: 18 cards

Page 34
Check students' work and reasoning. Briana needs 35 tiles.

Page 35
Check students' work. **Day 1:** 24 + 18 = 42 crayons;
Day 2: 9 × 6 = 54 players;
Day 3: 18 − 4 + 6 = 20 plates;
Day 4: 6 × 7 + 3 = 45 pepper plants

Page 36
Check students' work and reasoning. 32 ÷ 8 = 4, 4 × 2 = 8 minutes; Mateo needs to cook the meatballs for 8 minutes.

Page 37
Check students' work. **Day 1:** 3 × ? = 27, ? = 9 buttons; **Day 2:** 9 × ? = 72, ? = 8 chairs;
Day 3: 48 ÷ 6 = ?, ? = 8 stickers;
Day 4: 4 × ? = 32, ? = 8 tennis balls

Page 38
Check students' work and reasoning. 4 × ? = 80, Faith gave 20 dog bones away.

Page 39
Check students' work. **Day 1:** 4 fish;
Day 2: 40 stickers (5 for each bag);
Day 3: 21 pages; **Day 4:** 24 projects

Page 40
Check students' work and reasoning. Noah made $50.

Page 41
Check students' work. **Day 1:** no ($2.39 + $1 > $3);
Day 2: no (30 > 28); **Day 3:** yes (48 > 42);
Day 4: yes (6 pansies, 4 geraniums and 2 marigolds)

Page 42
Check students' work and reasoning. There are 8 girls and 2 boys in the music class.

Answer Key

Page 43
Check students' work. **Day 1:** 26 more passengers; **Day 2:** 300 more toys; **Day 3:** 50 meters; **Day 4:** 40 letters

Page 44
Check students' work and reasoning. Shawn and his friends planted 82 tomato seedlings.

Page 45
Check students' work. **Day 1:** 7 hours; **Day 2:** $14; **Day 3:** 8 buses; **Day 4:** 900 miles

Page 46
Check students' work and reasoning. Yes, they spent $9.54 and had 46¢ left over.

Page 47
Check students' work. **Day 1:** 6 cars; **Day 2:** 8 mice; **Day 3:** 8 paper clips; **Day 4:** 7 friends

Page 48
Check students' work and reasoning. There will be 5 amphibians in each habitat.

Page 49
Check students' work. **Day 1:** 54 ÷ 6 = 9 markers; **Day 2:** 56 ÷ 7 = 8 cookies; **Day 3:** 36 ÷ 4 = 9 players; **Day 4:** 40 ÷ 8 = 5 hours

Page 50
Check students' work and reasoning. 45 ÷ 5 = 9, The employees should put 9 fish in each tank.

Page 51
Check students' work. **Day 1:** Answers will vary but may include 465 – 343; **Day 2:** 24; **Day 3:** 90 more marbles; **Day 4:** Sophia is 14 and Ansley is 7.

Page 52
Check students' work and reasoning. Randy got 100 cards from his parents.

Page 53
Check students' work. **Day 1:** 24 cupcakes; **Day 2:** 5; **Day 3:** $40; **Day 4:** 7:10 a.m.

Page 54
Check students' work and reasoning. 16 brownies

Page 55
Check students' work. **Day 1:** 5 starfish and 3 crabs; **Day 2:** 24 options: JYDA, JYAD, JDYA, JDAY, JADY, JAYD, YJDA, YJAD, YDJA, YDAJ, YAJD, YADJ, DYJA, DYAJ, DJYA, DJAY, DAYJ, DAJY, ADYJ, ADJY, AYDJ, AYJD, AJDY, AJYD; **Day 3:** 16 outfits; **Day 4:** 18 options

Page 56
Check students' work and reasoning. The possible combinations are 357, 375, 537, 573, 753, and 735.

Page 57
Check students' work. **Day 1:** 5 boxes; **Day 2:** 6 yellow and 18 green candies; **Day 3:** yes, $80 left; **Day 4:** 240 stickers

Page 58
Check students' work and reasoning. Graham's mom will need to buy 16 bagels.

Page 59
Check students' work. **Day 1:** 135 sq. ft.; **Day 2:** 122 sq. yd.; **Day 3:** 74 sq. ft.; **Day 4:** 7,400 sq. cm

Page 60
Check students' work and reasoning. Cara will need to spend $72.

Answer Key

Page 61
Check students' work. **Day 1:** Rachel, by 1/4; **Day 2:** 13 pieces; **Day 3:** 5/8 **Day 4:** 10 slices

Page 62
Check students' work and reasoning. Yes, they both ate one-third of their sandwiches, because 1/3 and 2/6 are equivalent.

Page 63
Check students' work. **Day 1:** Xavier; **Day 2:** 3/4; **Day 3:** 3/5; **Day 4:** 1/6

Page 64
Check students' work and reasoning. Ashley should get 4 pieces of blueberry pie.

Page 65
Check students' work. **Day 1:** 50 hand-washings; **Day 2:** 690 calories; **Day 3:** 3 feet; **Day 4:** 14 minutes

Page 66
Check students' work and reasoning. She should estimate 150 minutes (about 2 1/2 hours) to finish her work.

Page 67
Check students' work. **Day 1:** Yes, he will have 12 cups of cider. **Day 2:** No, she will only have 32 cups of lemonade. **Day 3:** 8 cups; **Day 4:** Yes, she will have 40 pints.

Page 68
Check students' work and reasoning. Kedra will buy 21 feet of blue fabric.

Page 69
Check students' work. **Day 1:** 50 ft.; **Day 2:** yes, 21 < 24; **Day 3:** 28 ft.; **Day 4:** 3 m

Page 70
Check students' work and reasoning. No, he doesn't have enough glass (30 < 32).

Page 71
Check students' work. **Day 1:** 6 sq. in.; **Day 2:** Check students' work. **Day 3:** Answers will vary but may include sunflowers: 4 x 5, lilies: 10 x 5, daisies: 6 x 5. **Day 4:** They ate the same amount.

Page 72
Check students' work and reasoning. The largest dog pen would be 6 m by 5 m (30 sq. m). Also accept 10 m by 3 m (30 sq. m).

Page 73
Check students' work. **Day 1:** 12:00; **Day 2:** 8:10; **Day 3:** yes, 50 minutes; **Day 4:** yes (6:05)

Page 74
Check students' work and reasoning. Cindy can stop practicing at 3:30.

Page 75
Check students' work. **Day 1:** Yes. Rounding up, she spends about $50 with the earrings. **Day 2:** Yes. Rounding up, he gets to the rink at about 2:15. **Day 3:** Yes, they will spend about $16. **Day 4:** Ms. Rogers is right—she should get about $15 in change.

Page 76
Check students' work and reasoning. She has enough money to buy the box of tape rolls (about $80 + about $20 = about $100).

Page 77
Check students' work. **Day 1:** 146 g; **Day 2:** 6 kg; **Day 3:** 8 lb; **Day 4:** 600 lb.

Answer Key

Page 78
Check students' work and reasoning. They used 480 pounds of apples.

Page 79
Check students' work. **Day 1:** Sara/teddy bear, Morgan/sunglasses, Tina/fish; **Day 2:** Tia/apple; Tyrone/orange; Tanya/banana; **Day 3:** Erin is first in line (Erin, Nina, Hank, Ray; **Day 4:** dog/dish; bird/bell; cat/ball; bunny/treat

Page 80
Check students' work and reasoning. The cube package went to the green house, the sphere package went to the red house, the cylinder package went to the yellow house, and the pyramid package went to the blue house.

Page 81
Check students' work. **Day 1:** Answers will vary but may include a hexagon with 2-meter sides, a triangle with 4-meter sides, a parallelogram with 2-meter sides and a 4-meter top and bottom, a trapezoid with 3-meter sides, a 1-meter top, and a 5-meter bottom. **Day 2:** Answers will vary but may include a C or Z shape. **Day 3:** 48 yards of fencing and 11 fence posts; **Day 4:** 4 by 4

Page 82
Check students' work and reasoning. 48 ft.

Page 83
Check students' work. **Day 1:** 13 and 5, 10 and 8; **Day 2:** 28 or 82; **Day 3:** 9 and 1; **Day 4:** triangle and octagon

Page 84
Check students' work and reasoning. The boxes could be 9 centimeters by 4 centimeters.

Page 85
Check students' work. **Day 1:** Yes, they both get to eat 1/2 of the pie. **Day 2:** no, 2/6 = 1/3; **Day 3:** Shana's cracker was divided into fourths and Amy's cracker was divided in halves. **Day 4:** 3 whole candy bars with 1/2 left over

Page 86
Check students' work and reasoning. No, they both have 1/2 apple left, because 4/8 = 2/4 = 1/2.

Page 87
Check students' work. **Day 1:** Saturday, 405; **Day 2:** 7 hr. 50 min.; **Day 3:** 77°; **Day 4:** $1.05

Page 88
Check students' work and reasoning. Each bracelet will be 168 millimeters long.

Notes

Notes

Notes